NATIONAL GEOGRAPHIC

Where Is It Going?

Lee Scott

Where is it going?

37

Where is it going?

Where is it going?

AMBULANCE ONLY
PED XING
10 MPH
EMERGENCY ROOM ENTRANCE
AMBULANCE ENTRANCE
ONLY
Memorial Hospital
Service

Where is it going?

Where is it going?